Flamenco Music and Dance

Heather Hammonds

Contents

Music and Dance from Spain

Flamenco is a special kind of music and dance, from Spain.
The music is played on a **guitar**.
Singers and dancers join in.
They often clap their hands in time to the music.

Flamenco music and dance can be done by one or two people, or by large groups.

Flamenco Long Ago

Flamenco music and dance is very old.
It began in small towns and villages.
People sang songs and clapped their hands.
They danced to the songs.
At first, flamenco had no guitar music.

Soon, people all around the world
learned flamenco music and dance.

This painting shows people dancing flamenco long ago, in Spain.

Flamenco Music and Dance

Flamenco music is good to listen to.
Sometimes, flamenco music is soft and slow.
Then, it may become louder and faster.
The music sounds very exciting!

There are lots of flamenco songs.
Singers sing about happy times.
They sing about sad times, too.

Music played on a guitar is an important part of flamenco. Sometimes, there is just one guitar player. At other times, there are two or three guitar players.

Many people like to listen to flamenco guitar music. Guitar players strum the strings of the guitar. They tap their fingers on the guitar, too.

Some flamenco guitars have a special plate where players tap their fingers.

GRANADA

Flamenco dancers look beautiful when they dance. They stand up very straight and stamp their feet quickly.

Dancers must learn many flamenco dance moves. They can balance on one foot, or kick one leg up in the air! The dancers move their hands and arms in time to the music.

Flamenco dancers move their feet very quickly!

Some men are flamenco dancers.
Some women are flamenco dancers.
Children can be flamenco dancers, too.

Flamenco is a dance for everyone.

Sometimes, there may be just one flamenco dancer in a dance.
At other times, lots of dancers take part.

Often, there are many dancers in flamenco shows.

a flamenco show

Flamenco Costumes

Flamenco dancers wear beautiful dance **costumes**. Sometimes, people wear these costumes at a big spring **fair**.

Spanish flamenco costumes

Girls wear long dresses, or skirts and tops when they are dancing.
Most flamenco dresses and skirts have very bright colours.
Some have big dots on them.

Flamenco dresses and skirts have special **ruffles** around the bottom.
Dresses may have ruffles around the arms, too.
The ruffles on the dresses and skirts make the dancers look good.

Boys wear black pants and a shirt when they dance.
Many dancers wear red or white shirts and small jackets, too.

Flamenco dancers wear special shoes. There are lots of little nails on the bottom of each shoe. The nails help the dancers make a tapping sound when they stamp their feet.

There are nails in the heels and toes of flamenco shoes.

Dancers wear hats or other clothes
to look good when they dance.
Sometimes, they wave fans, or play **castanets**, too.

Where to See Flamenco

There are lots of places where people can see flamenco dancing and listen to flamenco music.

People can see flamenco at some Spanish restaurants.

flamenco at a restaurant

There are big flamenco shows all over the world. People can buy tickets to see the shows. Sometimes, there are flamenco singers, dancers and guitar players from other countries in the shows.

People like watching flamenco shows.

Learn Flamenco Dancing!

Flamenco dancing is good to learn because it is fun.

There are flamenco dance classes at some dance schools.

Dance teachers show students how to dance to flamenco music.
They teach them the special flamenco steps.

Flamenco is music and dance that everyone can learn!

Glossary

castanets *(noun)*	musical instruments that make clicking sounds
costumes *(noun)*	clothes people wear when dancing
fair *(noun)*	a place outdoors with stalls, rides and sideshows
guitar *(noun)*	a musical instrument with six or twelve strings
ruffles *(noun)*	frilly material sewn onto clothes